The **Cushing's Syn**

Stan Underhill

ISBN 9781453606643

Table Of Contents

Introduction: The Cushing's Syndrome Diet 1

Breads 3

BANANA AND WALNUT BREAD 4

FLOUR TORTILLAS 5

SIMPLE WHOLE WHEAT BREAD 6

WHOLE WHEAT PIZZA BASE 7

WHOLE WHEAT PUFF PASTRY 8

Breakfasts 9

FRUIT SMOOTHIES 10

GOLDEN WHOLEWHEAT CREPES 11

GRANOLA BARS 12

GREAT BREAKFAST BURRITOS 13

MANGO-BANANA-SPINACH SMOOTHIE 14

MELON BERRY SHAKE 15

RAW FRUIT JAM 16

SCOTTISH OATS AND FRUIT 17

TANGY BREAKFAST SCRAMBLE 18

WHOLE WHEAT PUMPKIN MUFFINS 19

Desserts 21

Apple, Cranberry, and Pear Crisp 22

Avocado Chocolate Dream Pie 23

Chewy Granola Bars 24

Chocolate Chip Cookies 25

Chocolate Crispy Bars 26

Chocolate Mocha Ice Cream with Saffron Cream Sauce 27

Peach Ice Cream 28

Raw Ice Cream 29

The Best Chocolate Chip Cookies in the World 30

Healthy Cookie Recipe 31

Tofu Pumpkin Pie 32

Vegan Cheesecake 33

Dinners 35

"Turkey" roast with wild rice stuffing 36

Avocado Burrito 38

Baked Mini Egg Rolls & Hot Mustard Sauce 39

Black Bean Chilaquiles 40

Black Bean Tostadas with Garlic Greens 41

Cashew Nut Roast with Stuffing 42

Chana Masala 43

CHEESY BEAN AND CHEESE ENCHILADAS 44

CHICKEN-FRIED TOFU 45

EASY ENCHILADAS 46

GENERAL TAO'S CHIKIN 47

INDIAN STUFFED PEPPERS 48

JAMAICAN JERK CHILI 49

KIDNEY BEAN BURGER 50

MUSHROOM PARCELS 51

ORANGE TOFU-CHICKEN 52

PAKISTANI DHAL 53

RED PEPPER, ARTICHOKES AND CHICKPEA FETTUCINE 54

SOUTHERN SOUTH SLAW WITH FRIED CHICKIN 55

SPANAKOPITA 56

STIR-FRIED NOODLES WITH BOK CHOY 57

SUPREME BURRITO PIE 58

THAI CHIK'N PIZZA 59

VEGETABLE FAJITAS 60

VEGETABLE KOOTU 61

VEGETARIAN LASAGNA 62

VEGETARIAN SHEPHERD'S PIE 63

WHOLEWHEAT PASTA SALAD 64

Drinks 65

CARROT LEMONADE RECIPE 66

CHOCOLATE SHAKE RECIPE 67

HOLIDAY EGG NOG 68

MINTY FRESH SMOOTHIE 69

PROTEIN NUTSHAKE 70

Lunch 71

"CHIKIN" SALAD WITH RYVITA CRACKERS 72

CHILEAN CORN AND "TURKEY" CHOWDER 73

CURRIED CAULIFLOWER SOUP 74

CURRIED SEITAN SALAD PITA POCKETS 75

EASY TUNA SALAD RECIPE 76

GRABANZO CROQUETTES 77

POTATO CARROT SOUP 78

SONYA'S FRENCH LENTIL SOUP 79

VEGETABLE AND QUORN SKEWERS WITH ROSEMARY-DIJON VINAIGRETTE 80

Salads 81

BLACK BEAN-AVOCADO SALAD 82

BOK CHOY SALAD 83

BRIT-ASIAN SALAD 84

CHINESE CHICKEN SALAD 85

CHRISTMAS SALAD 86

CRANBERRY SPINACH SALAD 87

DANDELION AND BITTER GREENS SALAD 88

FALL SALAD 89

FRUIT AND NUT SALAD 90

GREEN PEPPER TOMATO SALAD 91

LETTUCE, POMEGRANATES AND PINE NUTS SALAD 92

MEXICAN CUCUMBER SALAD 93

POMEGRANATE SALAD 94

SIMPLE CHICKPEA SALAD 95

SIMPLE SPINACH SALAD 96

TRINITY KALE SALAD 97

Sides 99

AVOCADO DIP 100

BLACK BEAN SALSA 101

BUTTERNUT SQUASH WITH WHOLE WHEAT, WILD RICE & ONION STUFFING 102

FIVE PEPPER HUMMUS 103

FRUIT SALSA WITH CINNAMON CHIPS 104

Greek-Mexican Couscous Salad 105

Mint Tabouleh 106

Spinach and Artichoke Dip 107

Vegetable Pakoras 108

Zucchini Cakes 109

Introduction: The Cushing's Syndrome Diet

Cushing's syndrome—your body's reaction to abnormally high levels of cortisol for a long time—is usually caused by the use of oral corticosteroid medication or an overproduction of cortisol.

As a result of this disease, you may be experiencing a host of unpleasant symptoms: fat deposits between the shoulders, a round face, stretch marks, slender legs and arms, and fatigue are just a few of the myriad of symptoms you might be experiencing.

While there are many treatment options for Cushing's, one is vital to insuring your overall health: a balanced, nutritional diet, low in salt and fat and high in protein and calcium. This type of diet can slow or prevent the loss of muscle and bone from Cushing's disease. Unfortunately, many of the protein sources in the typical America diet are high in both fat and salt, plus provide too much cholesterol for a Cushing's patient: many red meats, processed meats, and other animal products are all better replaced with healthier protein choices: beans, meat substitutes, and other low fat, low salt alternatives. Whole grains are a must and provide plenty of fiber. You'll find all of the recipes in this book provide you with maximum nutritional from plant sources— and yet the vast majority are quick and easy to prepare.

In addition to the diet recommendations in this book:

• Make sure you get plenty of vitamin D (a 15 minute walk a day in the sun will give the average person enough vitamin D. Depending on your overall health, you may want to take a vitamin D supplement).

- Exercise regularly. Include at least 30 minutes a day of aerobic exercise (a fast walk is enough), plus weight training to help prevent muscle and bone loss.
- Keep an eye out for diabetes—a potential complication of Cushing's syndrome. Symptoms of diabetes include increased thirst, increased urination, and fatigue. None of the recipes in this book are high on the glycemic index.

How To Use This Book

Start each day with one of the protein-rich breakfasts. A good breakfast, full of protein is an egg with Ezekiel 4:9 toast and butter.

Watch portions carefully. If you begin to gain weight (which, depending on your metabolism is quite possible), reduce portions or up your exercise routine to account for the extra calories.

Try the diet for one month. It will take this long to allow your body to adjust for the extra fiber intake. You may experience headaches or fatigue for the first few days as your body may rebel against the sudden reduction in sugary carbs. *This is temporary.* Once you have rid yourself of sugar and carb cravings—you're symptoms will subside to a more manageable level.

Breads

Banana and Walnut Bread

This delicious no rise bread is a favorite in our family. Make sure the bananas are slightly underripe so you don't add too much sugar content. You can find agave at Whole Foods or any health food store.

1	cup whole grain flour	1/2 tsp xanthan gum
1/2 cup oat flour		1/4 tsp salt
1/2 cup walnuts, divided		3 bananas (slightly green at
1 tsp baking powder		ends), mashed
1 tsp baking soda		1/2 cup agave nectar
1 tsp cinnamon		1/3 cup plain soymilk
1/2 tsp nutmeg		1/4 cup canola oil
		2 tsp pure vanilla extract

Procedure

1 Prepare an 8 x 4 inch bread pan by coating with grease.
2 Combine flours, walnuts (conserve 2Tbs for topping), baking powder, baking soda, cinnamon, nutmeg, xanthan gum and salt in a large bowl.
3 Place bananas, agave nectar, soymilk, oil and vanilla in a blender are process until just smooth.
4 Pour the banana mixture into the flour mixture and fold in.
5 Pour batter into the greased pan. Top with reserved walnuts.

Servings: 8

Flour Tortillas

This authentic Mexican recipe was given to me by a Mexican doctor who recommended it as a healthy alternative to white tortillas.

1/2 cup	vegetable lard	1 tsp	baking powder
4	cups whole wheat flour	1 cup hot water	
1	tsp salt		

Procedure

1 Put the flour in the bowl, adding the salt, baking powder, and lard, mix it with your fingers until it is crumbly.

2 Add the hot water -not boiling- , mix with your hands until you have a homogeneous, very sticky, dough. Add up to 1 cup more water if necessary (this will depend on the type of flour you use).

3 Cover with a clean cloth and let it rest for about 2 hrs.

4 Gently knead until smooth and separate into 24 equal pieces, knead the pieces with your hands until they are smooth again and cover again.

5 Heat the grill, extend one by one the pieces over a board with the baking pin to make round discs, lift carefully with your fingers and place on the heated grill.

6 Lower the flame to medium heat, leave for about 2 minutes -lift one end if it has a golden color you may turn it around to cook on the other side.

7 Once you do this, you may see that the tortilla inflates, depending on your own preferences.

8 You may leave it until it deflates by itself or push it down.

9 You may add some more fiber by reducing the amount of flour, 1 1/2 cups whole wheat flour and 1/2 cup of bran wheat, just remember that the altitude in your city will require adjustment of the baking powder.

10 To add more or less liquid - the batter should be firm, but moist, and with the standing time and the fat it should be elastic but not sticky; as with all batters, add a little more flour if needed.

Yield: 24 medium tortillas

Simple Whole Wheat Bread

I use a bread machine with this recipe. Just bung the ingredients in and go! I recommend you get one, otherwise avoiding supermarket breads will be a chore.

3	cups warm water	5	tbsp butter, melted	
2	pkg. active dry yeast	1/3	cup honey	
1/3	cup honey	1	tbsp salt	
3	cups bread flour	5 1/2	cups	whole wheat flour

Procedure

1 Place ingredients in a bread machine according to manufacturers instructions.
2 Bake on wholewheat cycle.

Yield: 3 loaves

Whole wheat pizza base

I cook all my pizzas using a pizza stone. You can purchase one for under $20; it's the difference between your pizza tasting home-made and authentic--pizzas off a baking sheet just don't cook the same way.

1	tsp	fructose	1	tsp	salt	
1 1/2	cups	warm water	2	cups	whole wheat flour	
1	package	dried yeast	1 1/2	cups	all purpose flour	
1	Tbsp	olive oil				

Procedure

1 Place all ingredients in a bread machine on the dough cycle.

2 Roll out to 12" circle.

3 See Thai Chikin Pizza for cooking instructions.

Whole Wheat Puff Pastry

The possibilities for fillings are endless: just make sure you use protein in the filling, as the pastry has a fair serving of carbs.

4 oz whole wheat flour
4 oz all purpose flour
1/2 tbs salt

3 drops lemon juice
very cold water

Procedure

1 Place flour and salt into a medium sized bowl. Cut the butter into 1/4" square cubes and add to flour along with the lemon juice.
2 Roll pastry into a 15" strip. Fold ends to the center, and fold in half again.
3 Turn pastry 90 degrees. Roll the air out with a rolling pin.
4 Repeat step 2 and 3 four times.
5 Best used immediately.

Breakfasts

Fruit Smoothies

Smoothies for breakfast are a staple in our house. The cashews and spinach add needed protein to make sure you don't have too many carbs.

2	Tbs	Flax seeds (soaked 3 hours)	1	cup	Frozen berry mix
1	cup	cashews (soaked 3 hours)	2	cups	spinach, uncooked
4	cups	water	1/4	cup	dates (soaked 3 hours)
1		Banana, frozen and sliced into 1" pieces			

Procedure

1 Place flax seeds, cashews, and water in blender.
2 Blend until well creamy.
3 Add fruit, spinach, and dates.
4 Blend until smooth.

Golden Wholewheat crepes

These thin pancakes can be filled with any fruit. Serve these pancakes with scrambled eggs to get the protein with this meal.

3/4 cup	wholewheat flour	1	kiwifruit, sliced
1/4 tsp	salt	1	orange
1/2 tsp	baking powder	4 Tbsp	orange juice
	enough soy milk to make a smooth batter	1/4 cup	honey

Procedure

1 Sift flour, salt and baking powder into a large bowl.
2 Add milk, whisking until a smooth batter forms.
3 Cook on a hot griddle until bubbles form and edges are light brown.
4 Peel the orange and remove slices. Skin, removing seeds and membranes.
5 In a small saucepan, put the orange juice and honey into the pan. Lightly boil for 4 minutes.
6 To serve, put one tablespoon of fruit in one pancake, fold over and drizzle honey syrup on top.

Servings: 2

Granola Bars

The trouble with store-purchased granola bars for reactive hypoglycemics is that they tend to be carb-heavy and laden with sugar. These bars are balanced. Make them on Sunday and they will last for a week in the fridge.

1-2	apples	2 tsp	sea salt
1 1/2	cups pitted dates (soaked for 3 hours)	7 cups	mixed raw nuts (coarsely chopped) and seeds soaked overnight and rinsed well (walnuts, almonds, pecans, hazelnuts, pumpkin seeds, sunflower seeds, etc)
1/2 cup	agave nectar		
2 Tbsp	lemon juice, fresh		
2 Tbsp	orange extract		
1 Tbsp	vanilla extract	1 cup	dried cranberries (apple juice sweetened)
1 tsp	ground cinnamon		

Procedure

1 In food processor, place apples, dates, maple syrup, lemon juice, orange zest, vanilla, cinnamon, salt, and process until completely smooth. Transfer to a large bowl.
2 Add nuts and seeds. Mix well.
3 Spread on a baking sheet and bake until crunchy.

Yield: 10 cups or 20 bars

Great Breakfast Burritos

Use the wholewheat tortilla recipe from this book for this breakfast staple. They can be frozen and microwaved for 2 mins to reheat.

1	12 or 16 oz	block of extra firm tofu, drained, pressed and crumbled	1	pinch	pepper	
			6		tortillas	
			1/2 cup		mushrooms, quartered or sliced (optional)	
1	ea	small yellow onion, peeled and diced	1	ea	jalapeno, sliced	
2	ea	garlic cloves, minced or pressed	1	cup	red, yellow peppers, diced	
			2	ea	Morningstar Farms breakfast sausage patties, diced	
1	ea	bell pepper, diced				
2	ea	small red potatoes	1/2 cup		cheese, grated	
4	Tbs	olive oil	6	Tbs	fresh salsa	
1/2 tsp		turmeric				
1	pinch	salt				

Procedure

1 Preheat oven to 375° Fahrenheit.
2 Chop your potatoes to bite sized or smaller pieces. Place in a Ziplock bag with 1T olive oil and a dash of salt and pepper.
3 Place in oven for 20 minutes.
4 While waiting for potatoes to cook, heat 3T olive oil in a frying pan.
5 Add garlic and vegetables. Cook on medium heat until the onions are softened.
6 Add tofu and turmeric.
7 Add sausage. Cook for 5 minutes, stirring occasionally until sausage is heated through.
8 Place warm tortilla on a plate. Fill with 1/6 of the tofu mixture and 1T of salsa.
9 Divide the cheese between the burritos. Roll up and enjoy!

Yield: 4-6 Burritos

Mango-Banana-Spinach Smoothie

While this green smoothie is delicious, it won't provide enough protein alone for breakfast. Try it with a slice of Ezekiel 4:9 toast or serve as a side for an egg and Morningstar Farms veggie bacon.

3	mangoes, frozen	1	Tbs	agave syrup
1	banana, frozen (use slightly underripe banana)	1/4	teaspoon	cinnamon
		4	cups	water
2	cups frozen spinach			

Procedure

1 Blend all ingredients in a blender and enjoy.

Melon Berry Shake

Serve with a heap of scrambled eggs and Ezekiel toast for protein. While tasty, this smoothie is too high in carbs to eat alone!

2   frozen bananas (peel and cut into chunks before freezing)
4   cantaloupe chunks
4   honeydew chunks
1 cup frozen blueberries
1 cup apple juice

Procedure

1 Place all ingredients in a blender and process until smooth.

Raw Fruit Jam

The perfect topping for pancakes or Ezekiel 4:9 flourless toast.

2 cups berries   1/4 cup agave nectar

Procedure

1 Place in a blender and process until smooth.

Scottish Oats and Fruit

This breakfast dish is served uncooked. Softening the oats overnight preserves more nutrients. I buy flax seed from a health food store: grind only as much as you need (I use a coffee grinder).

1/2 cup	steel cut oats	2	Tbsp	sesame seeds
	water	2	Tbsp	ground flax seed
1	large apple, cored and diced (do not peel)	1/3 cup		raisins
		2-3 dashes		ground cinnamon
1	pear, cored and finely chopped	1		banana, green at both ends, mashed
2	Tbsp raw walnut pieces	1	Tbsp	chopped nuts
2	Tbsp raw pecan pieces			

Procedure

1 Soak oats overnight in warm water.

2 In the morning, drain water from oats. Place in a glass bowl.

3 Place the bowl in a pan of very warm water and allow the oats to war.

4 Add the rest of the ingredients and stir.

5 Remove from heat.

6 Serve topped with mashed banana and nuts.

Servings: 3

Tangy Breakfast Scramble

This scramble will fill you up so much you probably won't feel like that mid morning snack! Nutritional yeast contains B-12 and can be found in health food stores.

For the sauce:			For the stir fry:	
1/2 cup	flour	1/2		onion
1/2 cup	nutritional yeast	4	strips	Morningstar Farm veggie bacon
1 tsp	garlic powder			
2 cups	water	1/2		green pepper
1 tsp	yellow mustard	6	ea	eggs, free range
4 tbsp or less	margarine	3	Tbs	olive oil
				Salt and pepper, to taste

Procedure

1 Mix flour, nutritional yeast, garlic powder, and water in a small saucepan. Heat on medium until thick and bubbling.
2 Remove from heat. Add mustard and margarine.
3 Saute onion and green pepper in 1T olive oil for 3-4 minutes until soft.
4 Add 2T more oil.
5 Add whisked eggs.
6 While eggs are cooking, microwave bacon until crispy (add 30 seconds to the suggested package timing).
7 Saute this for another couple of minutes.
8 Add salt and pepper to taste.
9 Add crumbled bacon, salt and pepper, and sauce from small saucepan. Saute for 2 minutes and serve.

Yield: serves 3-4 people

Whole Wheat Pumpkin Muffins

These are so delicious, you'll feel like you can eat more than one. You can find fructose in any health food store. It's a great substitute for sugar in baking.

1	15-oz	canned pumpkin	1/2	tsp	salt
3/4	cup	olive oil	1 1/2	tsp	cinnamon
1	cup	wholewheat flour	1/2	tsp	nutmeg
1/2	cup	oat bran	1/2	tsp	cloves
1/2	cup	quick oats	1	tsp	vanilla
1	large scoop	soy protein powder	1/4	cup	vanilla soy milk
2 1/2		tsp teaspoon baking powder	3/4	cup	fructose
1 1/2		tsp baking soda			

Procedure

1 Place pumpkin, oil, and fructose in a large bowl and mix well.
2 In separate bowl combine flour, oat bran, oats, protein powder, baking powder, baking soda, salt, cinnamon, nutmeg and cloves.
3 Add 1/2 cup of the dry mixture at a time to the pumpkin mix, stirring well between each addition.
4 Add vanilla and soy milk.
5 Fill muffin cups 3/4 full.
6 Test for doneness by inserting a toothpick into the center of the muffin. If it comes out clean, you're done.

Yield: 6 Large Muffins

Desserts

Apple, Cranberry, and Pear Crisp

This sweet treat is best eaten in small portions following a protein heavy dinner.

2	red apples - peeled, cored, and cubed	1/2 cup	wholewheat flour
2	pears - peeled, cored, and cubed	1/2 cup	fructose
		1/2 cup	quick cooking oats
1/2 cup	dried cranberries	1/4 cup	ground walnuts
1	tbsp all-purpose flour	1/2 cup	butter
2	tbsp honey		
1 1/2	tbsp lemon juice		

Procedure

1 Grease an 8" round baking dish with butter

2 Mix the apples, pears, cranberries, 1 tablespoon flour, honey, and lemon juice in the baking dish.

3 Combine the remaining ingredients in a small bowl and sprinkle over the fruit mixture.

4 Bake until golden brown.

Servings: 16

Avocado Chocolate Dream Pie

You won't believe that the base for this pie is avocado. Forget those supermarket, sugar-laden pies: this one's a dream!

2	large avocados	2	tbsp agave syrup	
2	cups vegan chocolate chips (try Tropical Source chips)		Arrowhead mills pie crust	
1/8 cup	soy milk	1/2 cup	frozen raspberries	
1	tbsp vanilla extract	1	tbsp orange juice	

Procedure

1 Sprinkle raspberries onto pie crust.
2 Melt chocolate chips in a microwave. Add soy milk, vanilla, and agave syrup. Mix well and cool in fridge.
3 While chocolate is cooling, peel and mash avocado until smooth.
4 Add orange juice to avocado and stir well.
5 Add chocolate mix to avocados. Stir well.
6 Pour over raspberries and place in fridge to set.
7 Top with whipped cream.

Servings: 4

Chewy Granola Bars

2 1/2 cups old-fashioned rolled oats
1 cup whole-wheat pastry flour
1/2 tsp baking soda
1/2 tsp salt, divided
2/3 cup chopped dried apricots
1/2 cup mini semisweet chocolate chips

1/2 cup chopped walnuts
1 cup packed light brown sugar
1/2 cup maple syrup
1/2 cup almond butter
1/4 cup vegetable oil
2 large egg whites

Procedure

1 Preheat oven to 350F. Coat 9x13-inch baking dish with cooking spray.
2 Combine oats, flour, baking soda and 1/4 tsp. salt in bowl.
3 Stir in apricots, chocolate chips and walnuts.
4 Beat brown sugar, maple syrup, almond butter, oil and egg whites with electric beater until smooth.
5 Stir in oat mixture.
6 Spread mixture in prepared baking dish, and pat down firmly.
7 Sprinkle top with remaining salt.
8 Bake 30 to 35 minutes, or until firm.
9 Cool 20 minutes before slicing into bars; unmold, and store in airtight container.

Yield: makes 25 squares

Chocolate Chip Cookies

Check the ingredients in the chocolate chips you use for this recipe: you don't want sugary chocolate chips that you find in the regular grocery store. Try finding carob chocolate chips in a health food store or dark chocolate chips, which contain less sugar. Grind the oats beforehand in a food processor.

1	Tbs butter	1/4 cup	canola oil
3/4 cup	rolled oats, ground	1/2 cup	fructose
1	cup whole-wheat flour	1	large egg
1/2 tsp	baking soda	1	tsp vanilla extract
1/2 tsp	salt	1	cup chocolate chips
1/4 cup	butter, softened		

Procedure

1 Prepare a baking sheet by coating with a thin layer of butter.

2 Place oats, flour, baking soda, and salt in a large bowl. Mix well.

3 Beat butter and egg until creamed.

4 Add oil, fructose and vanilla. Continue beating until well combined.

5 Stir in flour mix slowly.

6 Stir in chocolate chips.

7 Drop dough in 1Tbsp rounds onto a cookie sheet.

8 Bake until golden brown.

Yield: makes about 2 1/2 dozen cookies

Chocolate Crispy Bars

Why use vegan chocolate chips? They tend to be sweetened with fructose or evaporated cane sugar, which is easier on the blood sugar. But you can use any type of chocolate chips without sugar or high fructose corn syrup.

1/2 cup almond butter
3/4 cup honey
1/2 cup chopped almonds
1/2 cup vegan chocolate chips

3 cups crispy brown rice cereal (check ingredients for no sugar or high fructose)

Procedure

1 Prepare a 9" square pan by coating lightly with butter.
2 In a large saucepan, melt almond butter, agave syrup, and chocolate chips together.
3 Remove from heat.
4 Stir in crisped rice and chopped almonds.
5 Press into pan and allow to cool before cutting into squares.

Yield: 16 pieces

Chocolate Mocha Ice Cream with Saffron Cream Sauce

This recipe came from a raw food meet we recently went to. If you aren't familiar with raw food, the concept is that raw food retains more nutrients and actually makes you feel better. I'm personally not sure yet if the raw food lifestyle is for me, but I do know this ice cream tastes fabulous--and it's good for you! Our ice cream maker is a hand-churn style and we purchased it for less than $15 on eBay.

Chocolate Ice Cream

2	cups	coconut meat
2	cups	coconut water
1	cup	almond milk
1	cup	peeled Truly Raw cacao beans (powdered)
1/3	cup	mesquite pod meal
2	tbsp	Carob Powder
3/4	cup	agave nectar
3	tbsp	Coconut Oil
1	tsp	sea salt or to taste

Saffron Cream Sauce

1	cup	young coconut meat
3/4	cup	almond milk
1/3	cup	agave nectar
		pinch of salt
2	tsp	saffron

Procedure

1 Soak the saffron in 3 tbs. of soy milk. Let sit while preparing ice cream.

2 Blend all the ice cream ingredients together in a food processor. Strain through a wire mesh sieve.

3 Transfer to an ice cream maker and follow manufacturers instructions.

4 Add the remaining ingredients into the food processor and process until smooth.

Peach Ice Cream

Making ice cream (especially healthful ice cream like this) can be so much fun, you'll be doing yourself a disservice if you don't pick up an ice cream maker!

4   cups frozen peaches
1   cup vanilla full-fat soymilk
1/2 cup fructose

2   tbsp lemon juice
1/2 tsp   vanilla extract
1/2 tsp   salt

Procedure

1 Process all ingredients in a food processor.
2 Place in an ice cream maker and follow manufacturers instructions.

Servings: 6

Raw Ice Cream

1 cup raw cashews   1 cup frozen fruit
1 banana

Procedure

1 Place all ingredients into a food processor and blend.
2 Serve immediately.
3 Fold oil mixture into flour mixture, but don't overmix.
4 Pour into prepared pans, and bake 40 minutes, or until toothpick inserted in center comes out clean.
5 Cool cake in pan, then unmold.

To make Fudge Icing:

1 Sift confectioners' sugar and cocoa into mixing bowl.
2 Add shortening; beat 1 minute with electric mixer on low speed, or until well combined.
3 Add 2/3 cup boiling water and vanilla.
4 Beat until smooth and cool 20 minutes.

To make Peanut Butter Mousse:

1 Purée peanut butter and tofu in blender until smooth.
2 Blend in confectioners' sugar 1 Tbs. at a time, then blend in vanilla.
3 Chill mousse until firm enough to spread.

To assemble:

1 Place one cake layer on plate; top with Peanut Butter Mousse, then second cake layer. Frost with Fudge Icing.

Servings: 16

The Best Chocolate Chip Cookies in the World

3	tbsp	olive oil
2	cups	walnuts, ground
2/3	cup	fructose
2	tsp	vanilla extract
1 ½	cups	oat flour
1	tsp	baking soda

1	tsp	salt
1/4	tsp	ground cinnamon
2	cups	rolled oats
12	oz	vegan chocolate chips

Procedure

1 Preheat oven to 350°F.
2 Place olive oil and walnuts into a mixing bowl. Whisk (best done with an electric mixer) until blended.
3 Place and ½ cup water in a saucepan. Bring to a boil.
4 Add mixture to mixing bowl. Mix well.
5 Add vanilla, oat flour, baking soda, salt, and cinnamon to mix and continue mixing.
6 Fold in remaining ingredients.
7 Chill for 20 minutes. Roll out into a log shape (1" thick). Slice into 1" thick pieces.
8 Bake 10 minutes in a 350 degree oven

Healthy Cookie Recipe

Make sure you stick to the serving size (1) of these cookies. They are healthful, but sweet!

3		bananas, sliced and mashed (select bananas slightly green at one end)
1	tsp	vanilla extract
1/4	cup	olive oil
2	cups	rolled oats
2/3	cup	almond meal

1/3	cup	coconut, finely shredded & unsweetened
1/2	tsp	cinnamon
1/2	tsp	fine grain sea salt
1	tsp	baking powder
3/4	cup	vegan chocolate chips

Procedure

1 Combine bananas, vanilla extract, and coconut oil in a large bowl.
2 In a separate bowl, mix oats, almond meal, shredded coconut, cinnamon, salt, and baking powder together.
3 Combine the two bowls and stir well.
4 Add chocolate chips and stir.
5 Drop 1Tbs of the mixture onto a prepared (greased and floured) baking sheet.
6 Bake until golden brown.

Yield: 3 dozen bite-sized cookies

Tofu Pumpkin Pie

You won't have to go without pie this Thanksgiving with this hypoglycemic-friendly pie. You won't notice the difference--honest! The tofu adds protein, making it okay to have a slightly larger portion.

1	16-oz can pureed pumpkin	1	tsp	ground allspice, optional
1/2 cup	fructose			
1/2 tsp	salt	1/2 tsp		ground nutmeg, optional
1	tsp	ground cinnamon		
1/2 tsp	ground ginger	2-3 tbsp		cornstarch
1/4 tsp	ground cloves	1	10-12 oz pkg.	silken/soft tofu
		1	9-in	unbaked wholewheat pie shell
		1	pint	whipping cream

Procedure

1 Place the pumpkin and fructose in a food processor. Pulse for 15 seconds.

2 Add remaining pie ingredients and pulse until mixed well.

3 Pour pie filling into shell. Bake for 15 minutes.

4 Reduce heat to 350 degrees and continue cooking for 60 more minutes.

5 Best served cold with whipped cream.

Servings: 8

Vegan Cheesecake

I am lactose intolerant so cannot eat regular cream cheese. You'll notice no difference between a vegan version of the cheesecake and its sugary counterpart. Find Ener-G egg replacer in your local health food store.

1	ea	Arrowhead Mills pre-made pie crust
16	ounces	Tofutti Better Than Cream Cheese
1/3	cup	sugar (or fructose)
4		EnerG egg substitute "eggs"

1	tsp	vanilla
		juice of one lemon
1	can	whipped cream
		fresh raspberries

Procedure

1 Combine cream cheese, sugar, eggs, vanilla, and lemon juice in a blender. Blend until smooth.
2 Pour into crust.
3 Bake until set.
4 Cool, then place in refrigerator overnight.
5 Serve with whipped cream and a raspberry on top.

Yield: serves 8-10

Dinners

"Turkey" roast with wild rice stuffing

This fanciful dish makes a great alternative for Thanksgiving dinner. You can find tofu skins in Chinese food stores.

For the Roast

6-oz	tofu	
1	tsp	Chicken-style broth (e.g. McKays)
2	Tbs	water
3	Tbsp	plain soy milk
3	Tbsp	olive oil
1	Tbsp	soy sauce
1/4	cup	finely chopped onion
1	tsp	minced fresh garlic
1/4	cup	water
1	cup	wheat gluten
1/4	cup	besan
2	Tbsp	nutritional yeast
1	tsp	salt
1/2	tsp	freshly ground black pepper
1/2	tsp	dried sage
1/4	tsp	minced fresh rosemary
1/8	tsp	dried thyme

For the stuffing

1/4	cup	wild rice, cooked
1	Tbsp	nutritional yeast
2	Tbsp	vegan margarine
1/2	cup	finely chopped onion
1/2	cup	finely chopped mushrooms
1	stick	celery, finely chopped
1 1/2	cups	fresh wholewheat breadcrumb
1/4-1/2	cup	chicken-style broth (try McKays), dissolved in 2T hot water
2	Tbsp	dried cranberries, finely chopped
2	Tbsp	pecans, finely chopped
1	pinch (ea)	pepper, sage, thyme & rosemary

The "Skin"

16×20″ sheet		tofu skin
1	Tbsp	olive oil
1	tsp	soy sauce

Procedure

To make the turkey:

1 In a blender, place the crumbled tofu, nutritional yeast, dissolved bouillon, soy milk, olive oil, soy sauce, onion, garlic, and water and garlic into a blender. Blend until smooth.

2 Place tofu mixture, gluten, besan, nutritional yeast, salt, pepper & herbs into a breadmaker. Put on dough cycle.

3 Saute onion, celery and mushroom for 5 minutes. Add cooked wild rice, breadcrumbs, cranberries, pecans, thyme, rosemary, salt, and pepper. Mix well and set aside.

4 When bread machine has finished, turn dough out and knead, knocking out the air. Roll out into a 12" x 8" rectangle.

5 Spread the mixture evenly over the bread, keeping slightly from edges. Roll up like a jelly roll.

6 Bake for 40 minutes, covered.

7 Remove from oven. Allow to cool for 5 minutes. Soften bean curd sheet in warm water, then wrap over the loaf. Brush oil and soy sauce over the loaf.

8 Bake for 30 minutes more, turning half way through cooking.

Servings: 4

Avocado Burrito

These burritos will be bland if you use supermarket tortillas. Although the tortillas (see the recipe in the Bread section) take time to make, the simplicity of this recipe will more than make up for it.

3	avocados - peeled, pitted, and mashed	1	Tbs	olive oil
1/4 cup	onions, diced	2	ea	red and orange peppers
1/4 tsp	garlic salt	1	bunch	fresh cilantro leaves, finely chopped
12	wholewheat tortillas (see recipe in Bread section)			jalapeno pepper sauce, to taste

Procedure

1 Mash avocados together with onions and garlic salt in a medium bowl.
2 Cut peppers into thin strips. Lightly saute in 1T of olive oil for 1-2 minutes to soften slightly. Do not overcook--peppers should remain slightly crunchy.
3 Spread tortillas with the avocado mixture topped with the mixed peppers.
4 Garnish with cilantro and sprinkle with jalapeno pepper sauce.
5 Roll up the tortillas and bake uncovered for 5 minutes.

Servings: 6

Baked Mini Egg Rolls & Hot Mustard Sauce

You're playing reactive hypoglycemia roulette if you purchase egg rolls from a Chinese restaurant. They are high in carbs and contain unknown amounts of sugar. These rolls are more balanced with edamame and peanuts providing protein. They don't have hidden sugars--but they taste like the real thing!

Egg Rolls

1	Tbsp	soy sauce
1	tsp	rice vinegar
2	tsp	cornstarch
1	cup	shredded cabbage
1	Tbsp	sesame oil
1/2 cup		shredded carrots
2	cloves	garlic, minced
1	Tbsp	minced fresh ginger
1/4 cup		sliced water chestnuts, drained and chopped
1	cup	frozen, shelled edamame, thawed
2	Tbsp	finely chopped roasted peanuts
26		won ton skins
1		large cage free egg, lightly beaten

Hot Mustard Sauce

2	Tbsp	powdered yellow mustard
1	Tbsp	water
1	tsp	honey
1	tsp	rice vinegar

Procedure

To make Egg Rolls:

1 Whisk soy sauce, vinegar and 1 tsp. cornstarch in a small bowl.

2 Stir fry cabbage and carrots in 1 teaspoon of sesame oil for 3 minutes.

3 Add garlic, ginger, water chestnuts, edamame, peanuts and oil. Stir for one minute until heated through.

4 Add soy sauce mixture to pan and stir until thickened.

5 Prepare a baking sheet by spraying with cooking spray.

6 Place 1Tbsp of the mixture in the center of a won ton wrap. Fold one corner over the folling followed by two side corners. Finally, roll into an egg roll shape.

7 Place egg roll on the baking sheet. Repeat for all egg rolls. Spray lightly over all rolls with cooking spray.

8 Turn rolls after 10 minutes.

9 While rolls are baking, place all mustard sauce ingredients into a small bowl and whisk together.

Black Bean Chilaquiles

Short on time for dinner? These chilaquiles are healthful--and fast.

1	Tbsp	olive oil	1	Tbsp cilantro, chopped
2	cups	blue tortilla chips	1	green onion, chopped
1/2	cup	salsa	1/2	small tomato, chopped
1/4	cup	bell pepper, diced	1/2 ea	avocado (diced, for garnish)
1/2	can	black beans, drained and rinsed	1	cup cabbage, shredded

Procedure

1 Saute tortilla chips in olive oil for 1 minute.
2 Add salsa and peppers to pan, and stir well. Continue cooking until chips become slightly soggy.
3 Add remaining ingredients, reserving 1T of cilantro, scallions, and tomato for garnish. Continue to saute for 3-4 minutes until heated through.
4 Serve on a bed of cabbage. Garnish with chopped cilantro, scallions, fresh tomato, and avocado.

Servings: 1

Black Bean Tostadas with Garlic Greens

These are best with homemade tortillas, as you can get the small size (5")
that works best for tostadas.

2	Tbsp	olive oil, divided	4	cloves	garlic, minced
4		10-inch wholewheat tortillas	1	head	spinach, rinsed and torn into bite-size pieces
1	cup	diced red onion	1/2	ea	avocado (diced, for garnish)
1	can	black beans, drained and rinsed			
2	tsp	smoked paprika	1	cup	fresh salsa
1/2	tsp	dried oregano	4	Tbsp	chopped cilantro
			4	Tbsp	vegan sour cream

Procedure

1 Crisp tortillas by spraying a griddle with cooking spray and cooking
each side for 1-2 minutes.

2 Saute onion until softened. Add beans, paprika, and oregano.

3 Reduce heat to low and simmer.

4 Meanwhile, saute garlic in remaining oil until lightly browned. Add the
spinach and saute until wilted.

5 Assemble by spreading a generous spoonful of beans on each tostada.

6 Top with greens.

7 Garnish with remaining ingredients.

Servings: 4

Cashew Nut Roast with Stuffing

This unusual recipe makes for a delicious Sunday dinner when served with a selection of vegetables and roasted potatoes. You can find Marmite (a British product) in most large grocery stores. It adds a delicious tang to this meal, but if you can't find it substitute any other flavorful stock.

2	Tbsp	vegan margarine		2	Tbsp	wholewheat flour
2	sticks	celery, finely chopped		2	tsp	fresh mixed herbs
1		medium leek, finely chopped		3	cups	wholewheat bread crumbs
1 1/2		cups	hot water			Sea salt and pepper to taste
1	tsp	marmite				stuffing mix, prepared/packaged
3	cups	ground cashew nuts				

Procedure

1 Saute the celery and leek for 4 minutes in the margerine.
2 Mix the yeast extract into the hot water (alternatively you could use any stock you like) and add this to the leek and celery.
3 Stir in the wholewheat flour, nuts, herbs, breadcrumbs, salt and pepper to the water and mix well.
4 Prepare stuffing according to manufacturers instructions.
5 Place half of the bread and rice mixture into a greased 4" x 8" loaf pan. Press down with fingers to pack. Place the stuffing on top of this, topped with the remainder of the nut roast mix.
6 Bake for 40 minutes.
7 Sprinkle with fresh chopped parsely before serving and cutting into slices.

Chana Masala

Serve this delicious Indian dish with brown rice--stick to 1/4 of a cup of rice to keep the carbs down.

2 Tbsp	vegetable oil	1/2 Tbsp	lemon juice
1	medium onion, chopped	1/2 tsp	salt
			fresh black pepper
1 large clove	garlic, minced	1	Tbsp red pepper flakes
1 Tbsp	curry powder	1	Tbsp vegan margarine
1 Tbsp	tomato paste	4	Tbsp fresh cilantro, chopped
3 Tbsp	water		
15-oz can	chick peas, drained and rinsed		

Procedure

1 Saute onion and garlic in oil for 3-4 minutes until softened.

2 Add garlic, curry, and tomato paste; stir and simmer for 2 minutes.

3 Add chick peas, lemon juice, salt, and black pepper.

4 Simmer for 5-6 minutes.

5 Add red pepper and margarine. Stir through the melt the margarine.

6 Simmer for 5 minutes. Garnish with fresh cilantro.

Yield: 2-4 servings

Cheesy Bean and Cheese Enchiladas

You can use store bought tortillas for this recipe--they are baked in a tasty sauce so you won't be able to tell they were pre-made.

1/2 cup	cashews (soaked 3 hours)	4	Tbsp	margarine	
1/4 cup	wholewheat flour	10		wholewheat tortillas	
1/2 cup	nutritional yeast	2	small cans	enchilada sauce	
1	tsp	salt	3	cans	beans (white kidney, pinto, black), drained
1	tsp	garlic powder	2		medium onions, chopped
2	cups water				
1	tsp	mustard	1	can	olives, chopped
			1/4 cup		chopped cilantro, 1/2 cup salsa (optional)

Procedure

1 Combine water, cashews, flour, nutritional yeast, salt and garlic powder in a small saucepan.
2 Bring to a boil, stirring occasionally. When thickened, add mustard and margarine.
3 Heat on medium heat until bubbling and thick. Remove from heat and add mustard and margarine.
4 Add onion, beans, olives, cilantro and salsa to pan and mix well.
5 Divide the filling between the 10 tortillas. Roll up.
6 Pour 1/4 of the enchilada sauce into a, 8" x 13" baking pan.
7 Pour remaining enchilada sauce on top of the enchiladas.
8 Bake for 30 minutes until bubbling.

Servings: 6

Chicken-Fried Tofu

You won't believe that this is tofu! For an even better texture, freeze the tofu cutlets overnight on a flat pan. Thaw for 30 minutes before using.

1	lb	extra firm tofu, drained and pressed	1	tbsp	butter
3	tbsp	nutritional yeast	1	cup	soy milk
2	tbsp	panko breadcrumbs	1	pinch	freshly crushed black pepper
2	tbsp	soy sauce	1	pinch	thyme
1	Tbsp	Old Bay seasoning	1	pinch	oregano
1/4	tsp	salt	1	pinch	sage
1	tbsp	wholewheat flour			

Procedure

1 Slice tofu into 14" slices. Place in soy sauce and allow to soak for 30 minutes.
2 Combine nutritional yeast, breadcrumbs Old Bay, and salt.
3 Remove tofu from soy sauce and dip into the breadcrumb mix.
4 Place coated pieces on a oiled baking pan.
5 Bake for 30 minutes, turning once half way through cooking.

To make Creamy Gravy:

1 Melt the margarine in a saucepan. Add the flour. Cook over medium head for 2-3 minutes until bubbling, whisking constantly.
2 Add the soy milk gradually, continuing to whisk. Reduce heat to low, whisking until gravy is thick, bubbling, and lump free.
3 Add the pepper, thyme, oregano, and sage.
4 Stir well.

Yield: makes 8 pieces

Easy Enchiladas

This unusual combination of Spinach and Beans is tasty and full of protein and vitamins.

6	wholewheat tortillas	2 8oz bags	baby spinach
1 can	refried beans	1 8-oz can	tomato sauce
1 small can	chopped green chilis	1 16-oz can	sweet corn
2 can (6 oz)	enchilada sauce	1 cup	shredded Mexican cheese
1 ea	garlic clove, minced		

Procedure

1 Heat the beans in a pan on medium heat. When bubbling, add 1/4 of the enchilada sauce. Stir well.
2 Add corn and chilis to the pan. Mix well and turn heat to low.
3 Lightly saute spinach in garlic for 3-4 minutes until wilted.
4 Spread 2T enchilada sauce on a tortilla. Top with 1/6 bean mix, 1/6 spinach mix, and 2T grated cheese.
5 Roll up and place in an 8" x 13" baking dish.
6 Pour left over enchilada sauce onto tortillas. Sprinkle with cheese.
7 Cover and place in oven. Bake for 30 minutes. Remove cover for final 10 minutes of cooking.

Yield: serves 2-4

General Tao's Chikin

This kicked-up dish tastes wonderful with steamed broccoli and brown rice (limit yourself to 1/3 cup of rice)

1	package	Quorn chickin chunks	2/3 cup	vegetable stock
		1 egg	2	Tbsp soy sauce
3/4 cup		cornstarch	3	Tbsp fructose
4	Tbs	sesame oil		red pepper to taste
3		chopped green onions	1	Tbsp sherry, optional
1	Tbsp	minced ginger	1	Tbsp cornstarch dissolved in 2
1	Tbsp	minced garlic		tablespoons water
			1	Tbsp white vinegar

Procedure

1 Whisk egg in a small bowl. Empty Quorn into the bowl and toss to coat.
2 Sprinkle 3/4 cup cornstarch over Quorn, toss to coat (do not overtoss.
3 Fry Quorn for 8 minutes over medium high heat in a wok. Push to one side.
4 Add green onions, ginger and garlic to the center of the wok, cook for 2 minutes.
5 Add vegetable stock, soy sauce, fructose, red pepper and vinegar.
6 Add cornstarch to the center and heat thoroughly until bubbling.
7 Push the Quorn to the center and mix well.

Servings: 4

Indian Stuffed Peppers

The slow cooker will do all of the work for you in this dish. All you have to do for dinner is slice the tops from the peppers, remove the seeds, fill with the filling, and bake.

4		large red bell peppers	2	cups	cooked chickpeas
1	cup	chopped onion	1	Tbsp	minced fresh ginger
2	tsp	yellow mustard	3	cloves	garlic, minced (about 1 Tbs.)
1	tsp	cumin seeds			
1	tsp	ground coriander	1/4	cup	vegetable broth
1/2	tsp	salt	1/4	cup	chopped cilantro
1/4	tsp	cayenne pepper	2	Tbsp	chopped roasted cashews
2	cups	shredded green cabbage			
1	cup	diced sweet potato	3/4	cup	plain soy yogurt
			2 1/2	Tbsp	prepared mango chutney

Procedure

1 Place onion, yellow mustard, cumin seeds, coriander, salt, cayenne pepper, cabbage, potato, chickpeas, ginger, garlic, and vegetable broth in a slow cooker. Cook for 6 hours.

2 When done, stir in in cilantro and cashews.

3 Slice tops off peppers and remove seeds. Fill with slow cooker filling and place caps on top.

4 Place peppers in a deep baking pan. Place 1/2" water in the pan and cover with foil.

5 Bake for 40 minutes at 375 degrees.

6 Combine yogurt and chutney. Drizzle over peppers to serve.

Servings: 4

Jamaican Jerk Chili

So easy! Bung it all in the slow cooker...and enjoy hours later!

1 can	kidney beans, drained and rinsed	1		large onion, chopped
		2	Tbsp	vinegar
1 can	red beans, drained and rinsed	2	Tbsp	jerk seasoning (check for sugar content)
1 14.5-oz cans	diced tomatoes	1/2	cup	water
		1	Tbsp	fructose
1 14.5-oz cans	tomato purée	1/4-1/2	tsp	minced
4 ea	red potatoes, cut into bite-sized pieces			Scotch bonnet or habanero chile, or to
1 8-oz pkg.	vegetarian meat crumbles			taste

Procedure

1 Combine all ingredients in 4-qt. slow cooker or large pot.

2 Stir in 1/2 cup water.

3 Cook for 6-8 hours on low.

Servings: 8

Kidney Bean Burger

Use Ezekiel 4:9 buns for this burger (available in health food stores), and serve with a garden salad.

2	cans	kidney beans, drained and rinsed well	1	Tbsp	cayenne pepper
1		onion	1	ea	egg
2	cloves	garlic	1/2 tsp		oregano
3/4 cup		wholewheat bread crumbs	1/2 tsp		salt
1/8 cup		wholewheat flour	1	spray	olive oil
1	Tbsp	tomato paste			

Procedure

1 Chop garlic and onion in a food processor. Add the rest of the ingredients and process until blended.

2 Divide into 6 balls. Flatten into 1/2" patties.

3 Spray a frying pan with olive oil.

4 Cook on medium 4-5 minutes each side.

Servings: 6

Mushroom Parcels

You'll want to save these for a special occasion, like a birthday or holiday dinner. Save a little time by purchasing the brown rice ready made from the frozen food section.

1 cup	cooked brown rice	1		onion finely chopped
1	onion, finely chopped	1	cup	rolled oats
	cloves garlic, crushed or finely chopped	1/2 cup		butter
		1/8 tsp		pepper
1 jar	antipasto mushrooms, minus a tbsp mushrooms (make sure they are vegan), drain and reserve the oil.	1/8 tsp		salt
		1/8 cup		water
		1	tsp	mixed Italian herbs
		8	ea	fresh basil leaves
1 cup	chestnut mushrooms, chopped	2	Tbsp	tomato paste
1 cup	portobello mushrooms, chopped	1	recipe	wholewheat puff pastry (see Breads section for recipe) rolled into 4 x 8" squares
1 tsp	fresh oregano, minced			
1 tsp	fresh basil, minced			
1 cup	veggie burger crumbles, defrosted			
1 tsp	fresh basil, chopped			
1 Tbs	tomato puree			

Procedure

1 Saute the onions and garlic in the reserved mushroom oil until soft. Add the rice, mushrooms, oregano and basil. Mix well.

2 Place veggie burger crumbles, remaining Tbsp mushrooms, tomato puree and basil in a food processor. Blend.

3 In a small bowl, mix onion, salt, pepper, oats, herbs and water. Split into 4 and form 4 sausage balls with hands.

4 Put a sheet of puff pastry on a clean surface. Spread with 1/2 Tbsp tomato paste and top with 2 evenly spaced basil leaves. Repeat for other three pastry squares.

5 Spread the rice mix in the center of each pastry square in a strip. Top with the veggie crumble mix and finally the "sausage ball".

6 Fold up all four corners so that it forms a parcel. Brush with beaten egg.

Orange Tofu-Chicken

Serve this classic Chinese dish with 1/3 cup brown rice.

1/4	cup	cornstarch	1	Tbsp	lemon juice
1	block	extra firm tofu, drained and pressed	1 1/2	Tbsp	vinegar
			2	Tbsp	soy sauce
			3	Tbsp	fructose
6	Tbsp	sesame oil, divided	1/2	tsp	red pepper flakes, or adjusted to your taste
2	cloves	garlic, minced	2	tsp	cornstarch dissolved in 2 tablespoons water
2		green onions, chopped			
1/4 cup and 2 Tbsp		water			
1	Tbsp	orange juice			

Procedure

1 Cut tofu into 1" squares. Drain well on a paper towel.

2 Using a sieve, sprinkle a generous layer of cornstarch onto the tofu. Turn, making sure all sides of the tofu are coated evenly.

3 Fry tofu cubes over medium heat in 4T of the sesame oil. Turn, browning all sides.

4 While tofu is cooking, saute garlic and green onions in 1 tablespoon oil until garlic is light brown.

5 Add water, orange juice, lemon juice, vinegar, soy sauce, fructose, and pepper flakes to the pan.

6 Bring liquid to a boil; reduce heat to simmer.

7 Add cornstarch mixture into sauce, stirring constantly until liquid thickens.

8 Remove from heat and combine with tofu until coated.

Yield: 1-2 servings

Pakistani Dhal

Make the slow cooker do the work! Bung all the ingredients in the
cooker in the morning, and by the evening you'll have a tasty dal. Serve
with 1/3 cup brown rice or a wholewheat flat bread (a paratha, available
from Indian grocery stores)

1	cup	dry red lentils	2		tsp curry powder
3	cups	water	1/4	tsp	red chili powder
1		onion, diced	1		tsp ground cumin
2-3	cloves	diced or crushed garlic	1		tsp ground coriander
1/2		peeled and chopped ginger root			Salt and pepper, to taste]
1/2	can	chopped tomatoes			

Procedure

1 Place all ingredients in a slow cooker on low for 6-8 hours.

Yield: 4-6 servings

Red Pepper, Artichokes and Chickpea Fettucine

You can toast your own seeds and nuts for this fettuccine by dry-roasting in a skillet for 3-4 minutes.

1/2 cup	whole, toasted almonds		1	15-oz can	chickpeas, drained and rinsed
1/4 cup	toasted sesame seeds		1/2 cup		water, hot
1	ea	red peppers	1	9-oz jar	water-packed artichoke hearts, quartered (about 8 hearts)
5	Tbsp	olive oil			
1	Tbsp	red wine vinegar			
1	Tbsp	fresh lemon juice	1	pinch	pepper
1	tsp	cayenne pepper	1	pinch	salt
1	lb	wholewheat fettuccine	1/4 cup		chopped parsley

Procedure

1 Cut peppers into very thin strips.
2 Blend 1/2 of the pepper strips with almonds, oil, vinegar, lemon juice, cayenne and sesame seeds in a food processor until smooth.
3 Cook pasta according to package directions: drain and return to pan.
4 Combine all ingredients together in pan and toss well.

Servings: 6

Southern South Slaw with Fried Chickin

I found crispy chikin strips (made from tofu) in the freezer section of my local grocery store. Two major brands now make southern-style chikin from tofu and other vegetarian ingredients. None of the fat, and all of the flavor.

1	package	Frozen Southern Fried Chikin
2		medium carrots, grated
4	cups	green cabbage, thinly sliced
1/4 cup		red onion, thinly sliced
1	cup	red bell pepper seeded and sliced
3	tbsp	Vegenaise

2	tbsp	whole-grain mustard
1	tbsp	cider vinegar
1	tbsp	fructose
1/2 tsp		salt
1/4 tsp		cayenne pepper
1/2 cup		parsley, chopped

Procedure

1 Bake chickin according to package directions.
2 Combine cabbage, carrots, and bell pepper in large bowl.
3 Place Vegenaise, mustard, cider vinegar, fructose, salt, and cayenne pepper in small bowl and whisk until blended.
4 Combine mayo and cabbage mix in a large bowl. Combine well.
5 Chill for 1 hour before serving.
6 Sprinkle with parsley as a garnish.

Servings: 8

Spanakopita

The tofu in the spanikopita provides a healthy dash of protein without the fat (which you'll get more than enough of from the pastry). The pastry is half the amount that you'll usually find in this type of pie, to cut down the carbs.

1		yellow onion, finely chopped	1 Tbsp	lemon juice
2		green onions, thinly sliced	1/4 tsp	pepper
2	Tbsp	olive oil	1/4 tsp	salt
10	oz	fresh spinach	8 oz	frozen phyllo dough
1	pkg.	extra firm tofu, drained	1/2 cup	melted margarine
1	Tbsp	fresh dill OR 1/2 teaspoon dried dill weed		

Procedure

1 Saute the onions in the olive oil for 3 minutes until softened.

2 While onions are cooking, crumble tofu in a large bowl.

3 Add dill, lemon juice, salt and pepper, onions, and spinach. Stir thoroughly to combine.

4 Spread the spinach mixture into a 9" x 13" baking dish.

5 Top with one slice of dough. Brush with melted margarine. Top with another slice of dough and more margarine. Continue until all sheets are used. Brush top with margarine.

6 Let stand 10 minutes before serving.

Servings: 8

Stir-Fried Noodles with Bok Choy

This is the proper way to cook tofu--full of flavor, colorful and firm.

2	Tbsp	sesame oil	1	tsp	minced fresh ginger
2	Tbsp	soy sauce	1/8	tsp	red pepper flakes
8	oz	extra firm tofu, drained and cut into 1/4" cubes	1	cup	matchstick carrots
8	oz	wholewheat spaghetti	1		medium head bok choy, cut into 1-inch pieces (3 cups)
2	Tbsp	olive oil			
3	cloves	garlic, minced	2	tsp	low-sodium soy sauce
			2	Tbsp	lemon juice

Procedure

1 Cook noodles according to package directions.

2 Stir fry the tofu on medium heat in the sesame oil and soy sauce for 15 minutes until slightly shrunken and firm.

3 Add garlic, ginger, red pepper flakes, and carrot. Cook for one minutes.

4 Add bok choy, and stir-fry until wilted.

5 Add soy sauce. Stir well and remove from heat.

6 Sprinkle with lemon juice.

Servings: 4

Supreme Burrito Pie

It's the refried beans that add the protein to this dish. Refried beans aren't actually fried--the Spanish word refrito means "twice cooked" but was mistakenly translated as "refried".

2	cans	refried beans	2	oz	sliced black olives
1	container	fresh salsa	3	Tbsp	fresh cilantro coarsely chopped
1		tomato, diced			
2	cups	shredded romaine heart lettuce	4		wholewheat tortillas

Procedure

1 Place one tortilla on the bottom of a n 8"round casserole dish.

2 Spread 1/4 of the refried beans and 1/4 of the salsa on the tortilla.

3 Continue layering the tortilla, refried beans and salsa. Finish with a layer of beans and salsa.

4 Bake in the oven at 450 degrees for about 20 minutes.

5 Garnish with the remaining ingredients.

Yield: serves 4-8

Thai Chik'n Pizza

You can purchase tamarind from Indian or oriental grocery stores.

1/4	cup	peanut butter
1	Tbsp	soy sauce
1	Tbsp	chili paste
1	Tbsp	fructose
2 1/4	tsp	tamarind paste
1	clove	garlic
1/2	tsp	curry powder
1/4	tsp	sesame oil

1/4	tsp	grated fresh ginger
1	recipe	wholewheat pizza dough (see Breads section for recipe)
4		white button mushrooms, thinly sliced
3/4	cup	diced Quorn chickin
1/2	cup	diced red bell pepper
1	ea	small shallot, diced
1/3	cup	chopped cilantro leaves for garnish

Procedure

1 Put peanut butter, tamari, soy sauce, fructose, tamarind, garlic, curry powder, oil, and ginger in blender. Blend until just creamy.
2 Sprinkle a pizza stone with cornflour and place the pizza dough on it.
3 Spread peanut butter mixture over dough.
4 Sprinkle with remaining ingredients.
5 Bake for 25 minutes.
6 Garnish with cilantro.

Servings: 8

Vegetable Fajitas

You'll want to use the wholewheat tortillas from the Bread section for this Mexican classic. You'll need these tortillas warm before starting this recipe, so you are best using just-made tortillas.

8 ea	wholewheat tortillas	1		yellow squash, halved and sliced into strips
2 Tbsp	olive oil	1/2 cup	salsa	
1	red onion, thinly sliced	1 tsp	ground cumin	
1	green bell pepper, sliced	1/2 tsp	salt	
1	red bell pepper, sliced	1 cup	Mexican cheese	
1 tsp	minced garlic	1/4 cup	chopped fresh cilantro	

Procedure

1 Saute onion, peppers and garlic for 5 minutes.

2 Add squash, salsa, cumin, and salt. Stir well.

3 Cover, and cook for an additional 5 minutes.

4 Fill tortillas with mixture. Sprinkle with cheese and cilantro.

5 Roll up and serve.

Servings: 4

Vegetable Kootu

Kootu is aTamil dish, made from vegetable and lentils.

1	cup	brown lentils	1		medium sweet potato, peeled and cut into ¼-inch rounds
1/2	cup	fresh or frozen grated unsweetened coconut			
1	cup	cilantro leaves	2	cups	cauliflower florets
1/2	cup	lite coconut milk	1/4	lb	green beans
5	cloves	garlic, peeled	2	Tbsp	coconut oil
1		serrano chile, stemmed and seeded	1	tsp	mustard seed, ground
1	Tbsp	ground coriander	8		curry leaves
1	tsp	cayenne pepper			
2		medium carrots, cut into ¼-inch diagonal slices			

Procedure

1 Place cilantro leaves, coconut, garlic, serrano chile, coriander, and cayenne pepper in a food processor and blend until smooth.

2 Place the paste and all remaining ingredients in a slow cooker.

3 Cook on low for 6 hours.

4 Add coconut milk. Turn to high.

Servings: 6

Vegetarian Lasagna

This tasty lasagna is my kids' favorite meal. You won't even be able to tell there's tofu in it!

2	tsp	olive oil
2	cups	chopped onions
3	cloves	garlic, minced
10	oz	fresh baby spinach
24	oz	extra firm tofu, drained
8	oz	vegan cream cheese

1/2	cup	chopped fresh basil
1/4	cup	nutritional yeast
1	jar	Emerils' Kicked-Up spaghetti sauce
12		uncooked whole-wheat lasagna noodles
12	oz	soy sausage, crumbled
1	cup	shredded cheese

Procedure

1 Saute onions and garlic in the olive oil until tender.

2 Add onions, garlic, spinach, tofu, cream cheese, basil, and nutritional yeast to a food processor and blend until smooth.

3 Layer the ingredients in an 8" x 12" casserole dish in the following order: 1/4 Emeril's sauce, 1/3 of food processor mix, 1/4 sausage crumbles, 4 noodles. Repeat, finishing with a final layer of Emeril's and sausage. Top with cheese.

4 Bake for 30 minutes covered. Remove cover for final 15 minutes of cooking.

5 Remove from oven, and let stand 10 minutes before serving.

Servings: 8

Vegetarian Shepherd's Pie

This English staple is delicious and packed with just the right amount of protein.

4	red potatoes, cooked with skin on	2		carrots, diced
4 tbsp	butter	2	cups	fresh sliced mushrooms
	ground black pepper to taste	1 1/2	tbsp	wholewheat flour
2 cups	soy milk, unsweetened	1	cup	whole corn kernels, blanched
1 can	soy or Quorn crumbles	1	cup	Cheddar cheese grated
2 cups	chopped onion	3	tbsp	chopped fresh parsley
2 cloves	garlic, minced			

Procedure

1 Mash potatoes with 2 tablespoons butter or margarine, 3/4 teaspoon salt, and 1/2 cup soy milk until fairly smooth; set aside.

2 In a large saucepan, melt the remaining 2 tablespoons of butter or margarine over medium heat.

3 Add onions, garlic, carrots, mushrooms and crumbles; saute until the onions soften.

4 Sprinkle flour over vegetables. Stir for 2 minutes.

5 Pour 1 1/2 cups soy milk over the vegetables. Bring to a boil, stirring constantly to ensure a smooth sauce.

6 Simmer for 5 minutes.

7 Stir in corn, 1/4 teaspoon salt, and black pepper.

8 Prepare a 9" round baking dish by spraying with cooking oil.

9 Pour mixture into tip. Top with evenly spread mashed potatoes. Top with cheese.

10 Bake for 30 minutes. Garnish with parsley.

Wholewheat Pasta Salad

Thought pasta salad was in your past thanks to reactive hypoglycemia? Not so: the key is balance, and adding enough protein. Serve with a mixed green salad.

1	16oz box	wholewheat macaroni
4	tbsp	olive oil
4	tbsp	balsamic vinegar
1	ea	garlic clove, minced

1	can	black olives, sliced
1	can	chickpeas, drained and rinsed
1	ea	red bell pepper, chopped
1	ea	yellow bell pepper chopped

Procedure

1 Cook noodles according to package directions.

2 Cool, and add rest of ingredients. Mix well. Refrigerate until chilled.

Drinks

Carrot Lemonade Recipe

While this drink is healthful and tasty, you should eat it with a handful of nuts for protein.

4-5	medium carrots	1	round of ginger, about the size of a quarter
1	mildly tart apple (fujis or galas are nice)	1/2	medium lemon, juiced
1	1.5 - 2 " small wedge red cabbage		

Procedure

1 Place all ingredients in a blender. Blend until smooth.

2 Strain drink through muslim into a large bowl. Discard pulp.

3 Pour into a glass, and enjoy!

Chocolate Shake Recipe

You can drink this shake all on its own: the protein comes from the seeds.

2	Bananas, green at both ends	2 tbsp	Carob or cacao powder
1 cup	soaked, sprouted, brown sesame seeds	1 drop	hazelnut extract
2 cups water			

Procedure

1 Place all ingredients in a blender and blend until smooth.

Holiday Egg Nog

The trouble with regular egg nog is along with the eggs, you get a ton of sugar. This egg nog will delight you with just the right amount of spice and nogness.

5	cups	almond milk, unsweetened
1/2 cup	agave syrup, vanilla flavor
10	soaked dates
1/2 tsp	salt
1	tsp	tumeric powder

1/2-1	tsp	cinnamon
1/2-1	tsp	clove powder
1/4-1/2	tsp	nutmeg
1/2	tsp	ginger powder

Procedure

1 Place all ingredients in a blender, and blend until smooth.

Minty Fresh Smoothie

The addition of mint makes this a refreshing summer drink.

1 cup raw cashews, soaked for 3 hours

1   medium bananas

1   medium cucumber

2 tbsp fresh basil

1 tbsp fresh mint

1 ea   apple

Procedure

1 Put all ingredients in blender, and create a creamy and delicious smoothie.

Protein nutshake

You'll need a powerful blender to grind the nuts. If you don't have one, you can pre-grind the nuts in a coffee grinder. This makes enough shake for 4 servings.

2 cups	fresh pecans	2-3 tsp	agave syrup, vanilla flavor
8	pitted dates	1/8 cup	macadamia nuts
1 level teaspoon	sea salt	8	cups cold water

Procedure

1 Soak pecans for 10 minutes. Drain.
2 Place all ingredients into the blender. Blend on low, increasing speed until blended and frothy.

Servings: 6

Lunch

"Chikin" Salad with Ryvita crackers

This chicken-style spread is a no-cook dish that's ready in 5 minutes.

1/2 cup	raw sunflower seeds (soaked 3 hours)	
1/2 cup	raw cashews (soaked 3 hours)	
1/4 cup	ground pecans	
2	inch	piece of cucumber
1	Tbsp	onion
1		celery stick
1	tsp	dill
1/4 tsp	curry powder	
3	Tbs	lemon juice
1/2 tsp	salt	
1/2 tsp	black pepper	
1	ea	small carrot, chopped
8	ea	Ryvita whole grain crackers

Procedure

1 Place all ingredients into a blender and pulse for 2-3 minutes. Serve with Ryvita whole grain crackers.

Yield: 2-4 servings

Chilean Corn and "Turkey" Chowder

The slow cooker in my house is indispensable. Throw the ingredients on low at 7 am and it will be ready by lunchtime.

4 cups	vegetable broth	2	cups	chopped vegan turkey roast, or 3 frozen vegan chicken cutlets, thawed and chopped
1 rib	celery with leaves, chopped			
2 cloves	garlic, minced (2 tsp.)			
1	bay leaf	1/4 cup	flour	
1 sprig	whole thyme, plus 2 Tbs. chopped fresh thyme, divided	4		plum tomatoes, peeled, seeded, and diced (for garnish)
1	medium onion, peeled and diced (1 cup)	1		medium avocado, diced (for garnish)
1 lb	small white potatoes, diced (4 cups)	1/4 cup		coarsely chopped cilantro (for garnish)
4 cups	frozen corn kernels	2	Tbsp	lime juice, plus lime wedges (for garnish)

Procedure

1 Place first 9 ingredients (up to the turkey roast) in a crock pot. Cook on low for 4-6 hours.

2 1/2 hour before serving, dissolve flour in 1/2 cup water. Add to crock pot and turn to high. Stir well.

3 Cook for 30 mins on high.

4 Stir in tomatoes, avocado, cilantro, lime juice, cayenne pepper and lime wedges.

Servings: 8

Curried Cauliflower Soup

This unusual dish has its roots in British and Indian cooking.

2 Tbsp	olive oil	1 clove	garlic, sliced (1 tsp.)
1	small onion, chopped (1 cup)	1 large head	cauliflower, chopped into 1-inch pieces (6 cups)
1	medium tart apple, such as Granny Smith, peeled, cored, and coarsely chopped (1 cup)	4 cups	low-sodium vegetable broth
		1 tsp	honey or agave nectar
1 Tbsp	curry powder	1 tsp	rice wine vinegar

Procedure

1 Place all ingredients except for honey and vinegar into a crock pot.

2 Cook on low for 6 hours.

3 Blend 1/2 of the mixture in a blender and return to soup.

4 Stir in honey and vinegar just before serving.

Servings: 6

Curried Seitan Salad Pita Pockets

If curried seitan sounds unusual to you...just wait until you taste it. It's reminiscent of curried turkey.

1/3 cup	Vegenaise		1/2 tsp		pepper
2	Tbsp	mango chutney	1/4 tsp		salt
2	tsp	curry powder	2	Tbsp	currants
1	8-oz pkg.	seitan, rinsed and drained	2	cups	shredded romaine lettuce
1/4 cup	frozen peas, thawed		4	thin slices	tomato
3	Tbsp	red onion	4	rounds	wholewheat pita halves
3	Tbsp	salted roasted cashews			

Procedure

1 Combine first 10 ingredients in a food processor. Chop until mixture resembles turkey salad.
2 Place seitan salad, lettuce, and tomato in pita pockets.

Servings: 4

Easy Tuna Salad Recipe

Not tuna...but you'll think it is!

3/4 cup	raw sunflower seeds (soaked for 8 hours)	1	Tbsp	lemon juice
1/2 cup	raw almonds (soak for 8 hours)	1/2	tsp	dry dill weed
2	stalks celery chopped	1/8	tsp	celery seed
1	clove garlic minced	1-2	Tbsp	olive oil

Procedure

1 Place all ingredients in the food processor with the S blade and process until the mixture resembles tuna salad.

Servings: 4

Grabanzo Croquettes

I grew up loving potato croquettes (a thing of the past with reactive hypolycemia!). These protein-packed cakes are wonderful served with a green salad.

2	cans	garbanzo beans, drained	1	Tbsp	ground coriander
1/2 cup		wholegrain breadcrumbs	1	Tbsp	ground cumin
1/4 cup		olive oil	3		cloves garlic, minced
1	pinch	black pepper	3	Tbsp	fresh parsley, chopped
1	pinch	salt	1/2 cup		whole wheat flour
8		sun-dried tomatoes, drained and finely chopped	2	Tbsp	canola oil for frying

Procedure

1 Place all ingredients except for the flour in a food processor and pulse until well mixed.
2 Divide into 18 portions and roll into mini logs.
3 Place flour into a small bowl and dip croquettes into the flour.
4 Shallow fry croquettes in oil on medium heat until golden brown.

Servings: 6

Potato Carrot Soup

A slow cooker delight--packed with nutrients.

2	small cloves	garlic, finely chopped	1/2 tsp oregano
1		medium onion, chopped	1/2 tsp garlic powder
2		celery sticks, chopped	1 cup red lentils
2-3		large carrots, chopped	2 tsp McKays chicken-style broth or vegetable broth
4		smalll potatoes, cubed	2 cups water
1/2 tsp		basil, chopped	

Procedure

1 Place all ingredients in a slow cooker for 6 hours on low.

Servings: 2

Sonya's French Lentil Soup

I make enough of this delicious soup to freeze several portions.

1		large onion, diced	16-oz		dried lentils, sorted and rinsed
2	stalks	celery, chopped	6	cups	vegetable broth
6	cloves	garlic, smashed	2	Tbsp	dried thyme or oregano
2		bay leaves	1	Tbsp	Dijon mustard
1	Tbsp	tomato paste			pepper to taste
1 1/2	cup	red wine			chopped spinach (frozen or fresh), fresh

Procedure

1 Place all ingredients in a slow cooker on low. Cook for 6 hours,

Servings: 8

Vegetable and Quorn Skewers with Rosemary-Dijon Vinaigrette

You'll find Quorn in the freezer section of most grocery stores. A distant cousin of the mushroom, it's packed with protein.

Rosemary-Dijon Vinaigrette		Vegetable Skewers	
4	Tbsp sherry vinegar	1/2 bag	Quorn chickin chunks
4	Tbsp Dijon mustard	2	small red potatoes, quartered and cooked
3	Tbsp small shallots, minced	24	sugar snap peas
2	Tbsp lemon juice	24	button mushrooms
1	Tbsp grated lemon zest	1	red bell pepper, cut into 1-inch pieces
2/3 cup	olive oil	1	red onion, cut into 1-inch pieces
2	Tbsp chopped fresh rosemary	1	medium yellow squash, cut into 12 rounds
		1	medium zucchini, cut into 12 rounds

Procedure

To make Rosemary-Dijon Vinaigrette:

1 Combine all ingredients in a small bowl and whisk together.

To make Vegetable Skewers:

1 Thread vegetables onto wooden skewers.

2 Place skewers into a baking dish.

3 Baste generously with the vinaigrette. Reserve 1/4 of the vinaigrette.

4 Marinate overnight in the refrigerator.

5 Broil vegetables until just blackened, turning once.

6 Brush remaining vinaigrette over the vegetables.

Servings: 6

Salads

Black Bean-Avocado Salad

This makes a great side dish to a breaded chicken-style patty.

2	tbsp	lemon juice
1	tbsp	whole-grain mustard
1/8 tsp		black pepper
1	pinch	salt
2	tbsp	olive oil
2	ea	Roma tomatoes, chopped
1	can	canned black beans, rinsed and drained

1	cup	fresh or frozen corn, thawed
1		avocado, diced
1/2 cup		diced sweet red pepper
1/2 cup		coarsely chopped cilantro
1/4 cup		diced celery
2		green onions, trimmed and thinly sliced (about 1/4 cup)

Procedure

1 Whisk together lemon juice, mustard, and olive oil in large bowl

2 Add all remaining ingredients, and gently toss to combine.

Servings: 4

Bok Choy Salad

2	ea	Quorn breaded chikin patties, cooked and chopped into 1/4" squares	3	tbsp	soy sauce
			2	bunches	baby bok choy, sliced
1/2 cup	olive oil		1	bunch	green onions, chopped
1/4 cup	white vinegar		1/2 cup		slivered almonds, toasted
1/4 cup	fructose		1/2 cup		chow mein noodles

Procedure

1 Mix olive oil, white vinegar, sugar, and soy sauce in a large bowl.

2 Combine all ingredients in a large bowl and mix well.

Servings: 4

Brit-Asian Salad

1	head romaine lettuce (shredded)		2	tbsp agave nectar
1	tomato (diced)		3	tbsp lemon juice
1	avocado (diced)		1/4 cup	Chinese fried wonton strips
1/2	cucumber (diced)		1/4 cup	cashews, toasted
3	tbsp onion (diced)		1	ea nori sheet, cut into very thin strips
4	tbsp sunflower seeds			sea salt to taste

Procedure

1 Combine all ingredients into a large bowl. Mix well.

2 Chill for 30 minutes.

3 Before serving, mix again for 2-3 minutes to blend flavors and soften the nori.

Yield: serves 2-4 people

Chinese Chicken Salad

If you can't find spicy chicken-style patties, use plain instead.

4	cups	romaine lettuce (shredded)	1 1/2	tbsp	rice wine vinegar
	3-oz	spicy breaded veggie chicken patty, cooked and sliced	1	tbsp	fructose
			1/2	tsp	salt
2	stalks	green onions, chopped	1/2	tsp	Chinese 5-spice
16	ea	grape tomatoes			Toasted sesame seeds (for garnish)
		Dressing			
2	tbsp	olive oil			

Procedure

1 Mix the salad ingredients together in a bowl.

2 Whisk the dressing ingredients together.

3 Combine and serve immediately.

Servings: 2

Christmas Salad

4	ea	hard boiled, cage free eggs, peeled and sliced	1 1/2	cup	cherry tomatoes cut into quarters
1	ea	Romaine lettuce, torn into small chunks	1 1/2	cup	white mushrooms, sliced
1	ea	red leaf lettuce, torn into small chunks	1/8	cup	balsamic vinegar
1	heads	Belgian endive, turn into small chunck	1/8	cup	olive oil
1/2	ea	English cucumber, chopped	1/4	tsp	ground black pepper
1	ea	red bell pepper, chopped	1	pinch	salt

Procedure

1 Toss all ingredients together in a large bowl and serve immediately.

Yield: 10-12 servings

Cranberry Spinach Salad

1 tbsp butter

3/4 cup almonds, blanched and slivered

1 lb spinach, rinsed and torn into bite-size pieces

1 cup dried cranberries

2 tbsp toasted sesame seeds

1 tbsp poppy seeds

1/3 cup fructose

2 tsp minced onion

1/4 tsp paprika

1/4 cup white wine vinegar

1/4 cup cider vinegar

1 Tbsp garlic clove, minced

1/2 cup olive oil

Procedure

1 Saute almonds in butter for 2-3 minutes.

2 In a medium bowl, whisk sesame seeds, poppy seeds, fructose, garlic, onion, paprika, white wine vinegar, cider vinegar, and olive oil.

3 Toss with spinach just before serving.

Servings: 8

Dandelion and Bitter Greens Salad

4	tbsp	chopped fresh tarragon	2	cups	baby arugula
4	cloves	garlic, minced (2 tsp.)	1		medium Belgian endive, sliced into 1/2-inch-thick rings (1 cup)
1	cup	lemon juice			
1/2	cup	olive oil	1		medium carrot, grated (1/2 cup)
1	bag	Quorn chickin chunks			
2	cups	dandelion greens, thick stems trimmed	1		small fennel bulb, thinly sliced (1/2 cup)
2	cups	chicory leaves, outer ribs discarded, leaves torn into 2-inch pieces	1/4	cup	thinly sliced celery
			1/4	cup	chopped parsley
					Dash cayenne pepper

Procedure

1 Place tarragon, lemon juice, olive oil and garlic in a small bowl. Whisk together.

2 Place 1/2 of the dressing in a Ziplock bag. Add the Quorn and shake well.

3 Cook the Quorn in a non-stick pan for 10 minutes until heated through.

4 Combine Quorn, dandelion greens, chicory, arugula, endive, carrot, fennel, celery, and parsley in large bowl.

5 Pour the remaining dressing on top and mix well.

6 Serve immediately.

Servings: 4

Fall Salad

Make sure you use the plain chicken strips in the salad, and not the Italian ones, which lend too much of a strong flavor.

	Lemon Dressing	1		fennel bulb (1 lb.)
1/4 cup	lemon juice	6		oranges
1/4 cup	olive oil	6	cups	watercress and/or mixed field greens (6 oz.), coarsely chopped
1/2 tsp	salt			
1/2 tsp	cracked black pepper			
1/2 tsp	ground fennel seed	1	small head	radicchio (4 oz.), thinly sliced
1	Tbsp cider vinegar			
	Salad	1/2		small red onion, thinly sliced (¼ cup)
1	can beets (plain, in water)			
		2	cups	Morningstar Farm Chicken Strips, cooked
		16		pitted kalamata olives, halved

Procedure

To make Lemon Dressing:

1 Combine lemon dressing ingredients in a small bowl and mix well.

To make Salad:

1 Toss lemon dressing with salad ingredients.

Servings: 8

Fruit and Nut Salad

1	cup	slivered almonds	
1/3	cup	fructose	
1/2	cup	olive oil	
1/4	cup	distilled white vinegar	
1	pinch (ea)	salt and pepper	
1/2	head	iceberg lettuce, chopped	
1/2	head	romaine lettuce, chopped	

1 cup chopped celery

1/4 cup chopped fresh chives

1/2 cup dried, unsweetened cranberries

1/4 cup mandarin orange segments (in juice, not syrup), drained

1/4 cup sliced fresh peaches

1/4 cup chopped fresh strawberries

Procedure

1 Combine almonds and fructose in a frying pan. Cook over medium heat until almonds are coated and fructose begins to brown. Remove almonds with a slotted spoon.

2 Mix the olive oil, vinegar, 2 tablespoons fructose, salt, and pepper in a small bowl.

3 Mix all ingredients together in a large bowl. Toss well and serve.

Servings: 8

Green Pepper Tomato Salad

This tangy salad can be served as a side dish. Serve on a bed of lettuce for a full meal.

3	medium tomatoes, seeded and chopped		2	tbsp cider vinegar
1	medium green pepper, chopped		1	tbsp fructose
1	celery rib, thinly sliced		1/2 tsp	salt
1	cup chick peas, drained and rinsed		1/8 tsp	pepper
1/2 cup chopped red onion				

Procedure

1 Combine first five ingredients in a bowl.

2 Mix last four ingredients in a small bowl.

3 Combine all ingredients. Chill in refrigerator for 1 hour before serving.

Servings: 6

Lettuce, Pomegranates and Pine Nuts Salad

1/2 cup	cashews, roasted		1/2 tbsp	olive oil
3 tbsp	pine nuts		1/2	avocado, cuned
2 cups	baby spinach		1/4 cup	Pomegranate seeds
5 cups	romaine lettuce, torn		2 tbsp	Lemon juice
1 ea	garlic clove, thinly sliced		1 pinch	salt

Procedure

1 Combine all ingredients in a large bowl and toss well.

Mexican Cucumber Salad

1	can	black beans	1	tbsp	crushed red pepper flakes
1		medium cucumber, chopped	1/2	tsp	garlic, minced
1	can	whole kernel corn, drained	1/2	tsp	cumin
4	ea	Roma tomatoes, chopped	1/4	tsp	dried cilantro
1		green bell pepper, chopped	1/4	tsp	salt
1		red bell pepper, chopped	1/8	tsp	ground black pepper
2	tbsp	red wine vinegar			

Procedure

1 Combine all ingredients in a bowl and mix well.

2 Cover, and chill at least 1 hour before serving.

Servings: 6

Pomegranate Salad

If pomegranate is out of season, substitute papaya seeds instead.

3	cups	assorted baby lettuces	
1	bunch	watercress, stems removed	
1/2 cup		grapefruit slices	
1		small avocado, peeled, pitted, and cut into 1/2-inch cubes	
1		small red papaya, peeled and cut in half (reserve seeds)	
4	ea	hard boiled eggs	
1		small red onion, skin removed and sliced into 1/8-inch-thick rounds	

Vinaigrette

5	tbsp	olive oil
5	tsp	lemon juice
5	tsp	orange juice
1/2 tbsp		agave nectar
1/2 tsp		sea salt
		Seeds from 1 pomegranate
		freshly ground black pepper

Procedure

To make the salad:

1 Place all the baby lettuces, and watercress in a large bowl, and toss to combine.

2 Transfer to a serving platter.

3 Cut both ends from the grapefruit.

4 Starting at one cut end, slide a Paring Knife between the peel and the pulp, removing the entire skin and the outer membrane and lift out the sections.

5 Arrange the sections down the middle of the greens in a row.

6 Place the avocado cubes to one side of the grapefruit sections.

7 Remove the seeds from the papaya, and reserve for vinaigrette.

8 Cut papaya into 1/2-inch-thick slices, and arrange slices on other side of the grapefruit sections, top with onion rounds.

9 Drizzle the vinaigrette over the entire salad, and serve immediately.

To make the vinaigrette:

1 In a mixing bowl, whisk together 1 tablespoon olive oil and lemon juice.

2 Whisk in another tablespoon olive oil.

3 Whisk in orange juice and another tablespoon olive oil.

4 Whisk in honey or agave, salt, and remaining 2 tablespoons olive oil.

5 Gently stir papaya seeds into salad dressing.

6 Use immediately, or store in an airtight container in the refrigerator for up to 1 day.

Simple Chickpea Salad

1	can	chickpeas, drained	2 Tbs	parsley
1 1/2	cups	celery, diced	1 tsp	garlic powder
1/2	cup	vegan mayonnaise	1 tsp	onion powder
2	Tbsp	lemon juice		Salt and pepper, to taste
4	ea	Roma tomatoes	4 ea	wholegrain pita to serve

Procedure

1 Combine all ingredients. Chill for at least 30 minutes before serving.
2 Serve with fresh pita.

Simple Spinach Salad

2	cups baby spinach	
1/2 cup	blueberries	
6	strawberries sliced	
1/2 cup	chopped walnuts	

4	Tbsp	poppy seeds
1/8 cup		soy milk, unsweetened
2	tbsp	fructose
1/8 cup		venegaise

Procedure

1 Place first 4 ingredients in a bowl.
2 Place next 4 ingredients in a bowl with a tightly fitting lid. Shake, then pour over the salad.
3 Serve immediately.

Servings: 2

Trinity Kale Salad

8 leaves each of curly kale, russian kale and dino kale (shredded)

1 cup   cherry tomatoes halved

4 ea   hard boiled eggs, diced

1   tomato (diced)

1   avocado (diced)

3   tbsp onion (diced)

2-3 tbsp olive oil

2   tbsp agave nectar

4   tbsp lemon juice

         sea salt to taste

Procedure

1 Combine olive oil, lemon juice, salt and agave in the bottom of a large bowl. Whisk well.

2 Combine all other ingredients in the bowl. Mix well.

3 Chill for 2 hours before serving.

Yield: serves 2-4 people

Sides

Avocado Dip

Serve this dip with carrot chips and blue corn chips. Be careful with portions--you should eat more dip than chips!

2		avocados - peeled, pitted and diced
1	can	black beans, drained and rinsed
1	can	whole kernel corn, drained
1	ea	medium onion, minced
3/4	cup	salsa
1	tbsp	chopped fresh cilantro
1	tbsp	fresh lemon juice
1/2	tsp	cumin
2	tbsp	chili powder
1	pinch	ground black pepper
1	pinch	salt

Procedure

1 Place all ingredients into a food processor and process until just blended.

Servings: 12

Black bean salsa

1	can	black beans
1	ea	small green bell pepper, finely diced
1	ea	small red bell pepper, finely diced
1/2	ea	avocado, finely diced
1	ea	large tomato, finely diced

1/4	ea	red onion, finely diced
1	pinch	salt
1	pinch	pepper
6	Tbsp	lime juice

Butternut Squash with Whole Wheat, Wild Rice & Onion Stuffing

This makes an excellent side dish for a serving of protein (i.e. Quorn Chik'n).

4		medium-small butternut squashes (about 1 pound each)	1	Tbsp sesame seeds
			1/2 tsp	thyme
			1/2 tsp	marjoram
3/4 cup	brown rice (cooked)		1/2 tsp	seasoned salt
1	Tbsp	olive oil	1	cup fresh orange juice
1	cup	chopped onion		
1	clove	garlic, minced		
2	slices	finely torn whole wheat bread		

Procedure

1 Cut the squashes in half and scoop out seeds and fibers.

2 Place cut side up on a baking sheet and bake for 45 minutes.

3 Remove from oven to cool slightly. Reduce oven temperature to 350 degrees.

4 Saute onion and garlic until golden. Add all remaining ingredients to pan and mix well, ensuring rice is heated through (if cold).

5 Scoop out most of the pulp from the squashed evenly, leaving a "boat" with a 1/4" thick shell.

6 Chop the squash into 1/4" pieces. Stir into rice mixture.

7 Place squash and rice mixture back into the shells. Cover with foil and bake for 15 minutes until heated through.

Servings: 8

Five Pepper Hummus

Hummus should be a staple in any reactive hypoglycemic diet--it's packed with protein and is relatively low in calories.

1		large green bell pepper, seeded and chopped	1	16-oz jar banana peppers, drained
1	can (15 oz)	garbanzo beans, drained	1 clove	garlic
			1 tbsp	ground cayenne pepper
4		fresh jalapeno peppers, seeded	2 tbsp	ground black pepper
1/2 tsp		citric acid	1/4 cup	tahini
1/2 tsp		cumin		

Procedure

1 Place all ingredients into a food processor. Process until blended.
2 Serve with wholewheat pita bread or carrot chips.

Servings: 16

Fruit Salsa with Cinnamon Chips

This truly is a side dish: serve 1/2 a cup of the salsa and one tortilla with a large amount of protein such as a Quorn chikin cutlet.

2	kiwis, peeled and diced into 1/4" cubes	3	tbsp	100% fruit preserves
2	Golden Delicious apples - peeled, cored and diced into 1/4" cubes	10		wholewheat tortillas butter flavored cooking spray
8-oz	raspberries, quartered	1/3	cup	fructose
1 lb	strawberries, diced into 1/4" cubes	2	tsp	cinammon
2 tbsp	fructose			

Procedure

1 In a large bowl, thoroughly mix kiwis, Golden Delicious apples, raspberries, strawberries, 2T fructose and 100% fruit preserves.
2 Cover and place in the fridge.
3 Spray each tortilla with cooking spray. Keep in a stack.
4 Cut into wedges and place into a large Ziplock bag.
5 Pour fructose and cinnamon into the bag, shaking as you pour to evenly distribute. Close bag and shake well.
6 Bake for 10 minutes.
7 Allow to cool slightly, then serve with fruit.

Servings: 10

Greek-Mexican Couscous Salad

A true fusion dish! Try this fun recipe as a side to falafel or bean burritos (or, for an unusual combination--both!)

1/2 tsp	ground cumin	1/2 cup	chopped red onion
1/2 tsp	salt	1/4 cup	cilantro, chopped
1	tsp garlic clove, minced	1	small jalapeño pepper, seeded and diced, optional
1	cup whole-wheat couscous, cooked	3	tbsp fresh lime juice
1	can black beans, drained and rinsed	2	tbsp olive oil
1	cup frozen corn kernels, thawed		

Procedure

1 Mix all ingredients into a large bowl. Serve immediately or chill for 1 hour before serving.

Servings: 4

Mint Tabouleh

1 cup of cooked bulgur has 6g of protein, making this a nicely balanced dish you can also chow down on as a snack.

1	cup	bulgur
3	Tbsp	lemon juice
1/4	tsp	honey
3/4	cup	finely chopped pistachios
1	cup	finely chopped curly parsley
1		small English cucumber, finely chopped (1 cup)

1		medium tomato, finely chopped (1/3 cup)
4		green onions, finely chopped (1/3 cup)
1/3	cup	finely chopped fresh mint
3	Tbsp	lemon juice
3	tbsp	olive oil

Procedure

1 Cook bulgur according to package instructions--adding 3T lemon and honey to the water.

2 When bulgur is cooked, add remaining ingredients and mix well.

Servings: 6

Spinach and Artichoke Dip

The best accompaniment for this dip would be raw corn chips from your local health food store. These can also be found online. An alternative would be to serve with a selection of dipping veggies.

1   can artichokes, chopped into 1/4" chunks

1   cup cooked spinach, chopped into 14" pices

1   cup Vegenaise

1   cup Parmesan cheese

1/2 tsp garlic clove, minced

1/2 tsp garlic powder

1   dash hot sauce

1   pinch pepper

1   pinch salt

Procedure

1 Add all ingredients to a large bowl. Mix well.

Servings: 10

Vegetable Pakoras

These are a tasty addition to an Indian dish (such as a dal or curry). I use a Fry Daddy to fry veggies--if you use an old-fashioned pan, heat the oil to 375 degrees.

1	cup	besan	3/4	cup	water
1/2	tsp	ground coriander	1	quart	olive oil
1/4	tsp	salt	4	cups	assorted vegetables: cauliflower florets, green beans, button mushrooms, onion rings, thick slices of sweet potato, 3/4" carrot chunks
1	tsp	ground turmeric			
1/2	tsp	chili powder			
1/2	tsp	garam masala			
2	cloves	garlic, minced			

Procedure

1 Warm oil while preparing vegetables (if not already prepared)
2 In a large bowl, combine the besan, coriander, salt, turmeric, chili powder, garam masala, garlic, and water.
3 Mix well to form a smooth batter.
4 Toss the vegetables into the batter and mix well, ensuring vegetables are evenly coated.
5 Fry for 3-4 minutes until golden brown.
6 Drain on paper towels before serving.

Servings: 6
Yield: 4 cups

Zucchini Cakes

These make a great side dish to any protein.

2 1/2	cups	grated zucchini	1/4 cup minced onion	
1		egg, beaten	1 tsp Old Bay Seasoning TM	
2	Tbsp	butter, melted	1/4 cup all-purpose flour	
1	cup	bread crumbs	1/2 cup vegetable oil for frying	

Procedure

1 In a large bowl, combine zucchini, egg, and butter or margarine.

2 Stir in seasoned crumbs, minced onion, and seasoning; mix well.

3 Shape mixture into patties then dredge in flour.

4 In a medium skillet, heat oil over medium high heat until hot.

5 Fry patties in oil until golden brown on both sides.

Servings: 5

Index

A

Apple, Cranberry, and Pear Crisp 22

Avocado Burrito 38

Avocado Chocolate Dream Pie.............................. 23

Avocado Dip 100

B

Baked Mini Egg Rolls & Hot Mustard Sauce..... 39

Banana and Walnut Bread 4

Black Bean Chilaquiles.. 40

Black bean salsa 101

Black Bean Tostadas with Garlic Greens 41

Black Bean-Avocado Salad 82

Bok Choy Salad............. 83

Brit-Asian Salad 84

Butternut Squash with Whole Wheat, Wild Rice & Onion Stuffing....... 102

C

Carrot Lemonade Recipe 66

Cashew Nut Roast with Stuffing......................42

Chana Masala...............43

Cheesy Bean and Cheese Enchiladas..................44

Chewy Granola Bars 24

Chicken-Fried Tofu 45

Chilean Corn and...........73

Chinese Chicken Salad .85

Chocolate Chip Cookies .25

Chocolate Crispy Bars....26

Chocolate Mocha Ice Cream with Saffron Cream Sauce 27

Chocolate Shake Recipe .67

Christmas Salad 86

Cranberry Spinach Salad 87

Curried Cauliflower Soup 74

Curried Seitan Salad Pita Pockets........................ 75

D

Dandelion and Bitter Greens Salad.............. 88

E

Easy Enchiladas............ 46

Easy Tuna Salad Recipe 76

F

Fall Salad...................... 89

Five Pepper Hummus .. 103

Flour Tortillas 5

Fruit and Nut Salad....... 90

Fruit Salsa with Cinnamon Chips 104

Fruit Smoothies............. 10

G

General Tao's Chikin 47

Golden Wholewheat crepes 11

Grabanzo Croquettes 77

Granola Bars 12

Great Breakfast Burritos 13

Greek-Mexican Couscous Salad 105

Green Pepper Tomato Salad 91

H

Holiday Egg Nog............. 68

I

Indian Stuffed Peppers...48

J

Jamaican Jerk Chili....... 49

K

Kidney Bean Burger....... 50

L

Lettuce, Pomegranates and Pine Nuts Salad 92

M

Mango-Banana-Spinach
  Smoothie 14

Melon Berry Shake 15

Mexican Cucumber Salad
  93

Mint Tabouleh 106

Minty Fresh Smoothie ... 69

Mushroom Parcels 51

O

Orange Tofu-Chicken 52

P

Pakistani Dhal 53

Peach Ice Cream 28

Pomegranate Salad 94

Potato Carrot Soup 78

Protein nutshake 70

R

Raw Fruit Jam 16

Raw Ice Cream 29

Red Pepper, Artichokes
  and Chickpea Fettucine
  54

S

Scottish Oats and Fruit .. 17

Simple Chickpea Salad .. 95

Simple Spinach Salad 96

Simple Whole Wheat Bread
  6

Sonya's French Lentil Soup
  79

Southern South Slaw with
  Fried Chickin 55

Spanakopita 56

Spinach and Artichoke Dip
  107

Stir-Fried Noodles with
  Bok Choy 57

Supreme Burrito Pie 58

T

Tangy Breakfast Scramble
  18

Thai Chik'n Pizza 59

The Heart-Healthiest Chocolate Chip Cookies in the World 30

The World's Only Healthy Cookie Recipe 31

Tofu Pumpkin Pie 32

Trinity Kale Salad 97

V

Vegan Cheesecake 33

Vegetable and Quorn Skewers with Rosemary-Dijon Vinaigrette 80

Vegetable Fajitas 60

Vegetable Kootu 61

Vegetable Pakoras 108

Vegetarian Lasagna 62

Vegetarian Shepherd's Pie 63

W

Whole wheat pizza base ...7

Whole Wheat Puff Pastry ..8

Whole Wheat Pumpkin Muffins 19

Wholewheat Pasta Salad 64

Z

Zucchini Cakes 109

Apple, Cranberry, and Pear Crisp, 22

Avocado Burrito, 38

Avocado Chocolate Dream Pie, 23

Avocado Dip, 100

Baked Mini Egg Rolls & Hot Mustard Sauce, 39

Banana and Walnut Bread, 4

Black Bean Chilaquiles, 40

Black bean salsa, 101

Black Bean Tostadas with Garlic Greens, 41

Black Bean-Avocado Salad, 82

Bok Choy Salad, 83

Brit-Asian Salad, 84

Butternut Squash with Whole Wheat, Wild Rice & Onion Stuffing, 102

Carrot Lemonade Recipe, 66

Cashew Nut Roast with Stuffing, 42

Chana Masala, 43

Cheesy Bean and Cheese Enchiladas, 44

Chewy Granola Bars, 24

Chicken-Fried Tofu, 45

Chilean Corn and, 73

Chinese Chicken Salad, 85

Chocolate Chip Cookies, 25

Chocolate Crispy Bars, 26

Chocolate Mocha Ice Cream with Saffron Cream Sauce, 27

Chocolate Shake Recipe, 67

Christmas Salad, 86

Cranberry Spinach Salad, 87

Curried Cauliflower Soup, 74

Curried Seitan Salad Pita Pockets, 75

Dandelion and Bitter Greens Salad, 88

Easy Enchiladas, 46

Easy Tuna Salad Recipe, 76

Fall Salad, 89

Five Pepper Hummus, 103

Flour Tortillas, 5

Fruit and Nut Salad, 90

Fruit Salsa with Cinnamon Chips, 104

Fruit Smoothies, 10

General Tao's Chikin, 47

Golden Wholewheat crepes, 11

Grabanzo Croquettes, 77

Granola Bars, 12

Great Breakfast Burritos, 13

Greek-Mexican Couscous Salad, 105

Green Pepper Tomato Salad, 91

Holiday Egg Nog, 68

Indian Stuffed Peppers, 48

Jamaican Jerk Chili, 49

Kidney Bean Burger, 50

Lettuce, Pomegranates and Pine Nuts Salad, 92

Mango-Banana-Spinach Smoothie, 14

Melon Berry Shake, 15

Mexican Cucumber Salad, 93

Mint Tabouleh, 106

Minty Fresh Smoothie, 69

Mushroom Parcels, 51

Orange Tofu-Chicken, 52

Pakistani Dhal, 53

Peach Ice Cream, 28

Pomegranate Salad, 94

Potato Carrot Soup, 78

Protein nutshake, 70

Raw Fruit Jam, 16

Raw Ice Cream, 29

Red Pepper, Artichokes and Chickpea Fettucine, 54

Scottish Oats and Fruit, 17

Simple Chickpea Salad, 95

Simple Spinach Salad, 96

Simple Whole Wheat Bread, 6

Sonya's French Lentil Soup, 79

Southern South Slaw with Fried Chickin, 55

Spanakopita, 56

Spinach and Artichoke Dip, 107

Stir-Fried Noodles with Bok Choy, 57

Supreme Burrito Pie, 58

Tangy Breakfast Scramble, 18

Thai Chik'n Pizza, 59

The Heart-Healthiest Chocolate Chip Cookies in the World, 30

The World's Only Healthy Cookie Recipe, 31

Tofu Pumpkin Pie, 32

Trinity Kale Salad, 97

Vegan Cheesecake, 33

Vegetable and Quorn Skewers with Rosemary-Dijon Vinaigrette, 80

Vegetable Fajitas, 60

Vegetable Kootu, 61

Vegetable Pakoras, 108

Vegetarian Lasagna, 62

Vegetarian Shepherd's Pie, 63

Whole wheat pizza base, 7

Whole Wheat Puff Pastry, 8

Whole Wheat Pumpkin Muffins, 19

Wholewheat Pasta Salad, 64

Zucchini Cakes, 109